Bubblegum Delicious

Wrap you up in bubble wrap,
Wrap you up in gum,
Wrap you up in wonderful
'Cause you're the special one!

BUBBLEGUM delicious,
Bubblegum delight,
Bubblegum de-lovely in the
Middle of the night.

Published by HarperCollins Publishers Ltd

First published by Key Porter Books in a hardcover edition: 2000
First paperback edition: 2001
First published by HarperCollins Publishers Ltd in this hardcover Classic Edition: 2012

HarperCollins books may be purchased for educational, sales,
or business promotional use through our Special Markets Department.

HarperCollins Publishers Ltd
2 Bloor Street East, 20th Floor
Toronto, Ontario, Canada
M4W 1A8

www.harpercollins.ca

Library and Archives Canada Cataloguing in Publication information is available upon request

ISBN: 978-1-44341-159-2

Text set in Cartier
Design: Peter Maher

Printed and bound in Canada

DWF 9 8 7 6 5 4 3 2 1

Bless my booty, / Bless my soul— / Here comes bratty / Bug patrol!

Bubblegum Delicious

Poems by Dennis Lee

Illustrations by David McPhail

HarperCollins Publishers Ltd

Good Morning

When I woke up, my heart was high.
The sun was hot in the bright blue sky.
The bees were buzzing, and I knew why —
'Cause I had a friend to play with!

Well it's one-ery, two-ery, hickory, dock:
Dogs can dance and bugs can talk.
There's tons of secrets around the block —
And I have a friend to play with!

Round and around in the neighbourhood,
The day goes by like a daytime should.
So tickle my tummy and I'll be good —
'Cause I've got a friend to play with!

Bump! in the bathroom!
Jump! on the chairs!
Thump! through the bedroom,
And stump!

down the

stairs.

The Rocking Chair

I LOVE to rock
    In the rocking chair.
I rock rock rock
    And I just don't care.

I rock around the block
    In my underwear;
Then I rock back home
    In the rocking chair.

Flying

Fly me round the microwave.
Fly me round the moon.
Fly me like a millionaire
On a Saturday afternoon!

The Movies

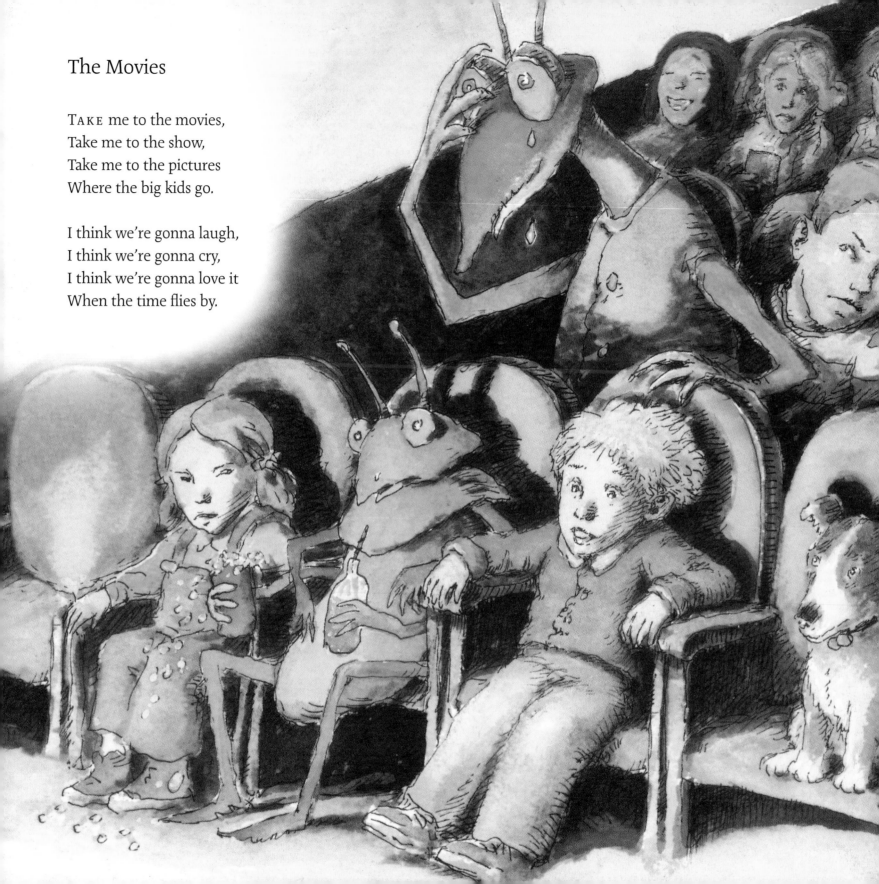

Take me to the movies,
Take me to the show,
Take me to the pictures
Where the big kids go.

I think we're gonna laugh,
I think we're gonna cry,
I think we're gonna love it
When the time flies by.

Mighty Hunters

THROUGH the city, block on block,
A pair of mighty hunters stalk.

Down the alley — hush! beware!
Tracking bad guys to their lair.

Past the hideout — not a peep!
Where the bad guys strut and creep.

Now it's time for an attack:
Holler *Charge!* and drive them back.

FLEAS FLY A LITTLE.
FLIES FLEE A LOT.
BUT I CAN FLY BOTH LOW AND HIGH
AROUND THE CHIMNEY POT.

Dipsy-doodle through the lane,
Turn around and *Charge!* again,

Till the bad guys in dismay
Spread their wings and fly away...

Through the city, block on block,
A pair of mighty hunters stalk.

Goober and Guck

GOOBER and guck,
Goober and guck,
We're making a sandwich
Of goober and guck.

It won't make you healthy
Or bring you good luck,
But gobble it down and
You'll quack like a duck;

You'll quack like a duck and
You'll smell like a truck —
So eat your nice sandwich
Of goober and guck!

People, people, don't be shy — / Step right up for your toe-jam pie: / (You get) one for a tummy-ache, two for a bed, / And three for a coffin when you fall down dead!

The Question

IF I could teach you how to fly
Or bake an elderberry pie
Or turn the sidewalk into stars
Or play new songs on an old guitar
Or if I knew the way to heaven
The names of night, the taste of seven
And owned them all, to keep or lend —
Would you come and be my friend?

*

You cannot teach me how to fly.
I love the berries but not the pie.
The sidewalks are for walking on,
And an old guitar has just one song.
The names of night cannot be known,
The way to heaven cannot be shown.
You cannot keep, you cannot lend —
But still I want you for my friend.

Dunking

ALLEY-alley-oop
To the basketball hoop:
Dunk it like a donut
With a holler and a whoop!

Four little beetlebugs, climbing up the wall:
One was George and one was Paul.
One was John, with his head between his toes,
And one was Ringo, with a pickle up his nose.

Pollywog Dreams

POLLYWOGS
  In parachutes
Are drifting through
  My dream —
Pollywogs
  In parachutes,
With pink and white
  Ice cream.

They move in cloud
  Formation
As they curtsey
  One, two, three —
Pollywogs
  In parachutes,
Above the maple
  Tree.

They never guess
  I'm dreaming them,
But in my dream
  I see
That pollywogs
  In parachutes
Are also dreaming
  Me.

The King of Calabogie

THE KING of Calabogie
Had a tickle in his throat.
He coughed a long and mighty cough,
And up came — a goat!

The goat the king provoked began
To butt His Highness flat.
It horked a long and mighty hork,
And up came — a cat!

The cat the goat begat began
To guzzle apple juice.
It burped a long and mighty burp,
And up came — a goose!

The goose the cat produced began
To flap like anything.
It honked a long and mighty honk,
And up came — a king!

The Spider's Web

THE SUN upon a spider's web
    Makes jewels in the air,
As though the light was tangled up
    In someone's windy hair,

Or in a flight of skipping-stones
    Across a river's flare,
Or in a mind of many thoughts,
    Whose owner isn't there.

The Waves

THEY'RE old, they're old, they're very old,
    As old as evermore,
The long blue slap and the sucking waves
    That pound against the shore.

And starfish and anemones
    Go trundling to and fro,
Like starfish and anemones
    A million years ago.

And the waves roll in, and the tides roll in,
    And the sea rolls in each day.
And people for a thousand years
    Have heard the ocean say,

We're old, we're old, we're very old,
    As old as evermore,
The long blue slap and the sucking waves
    That pound against the shore.

Doctor Bop

THE BAND was playing dixie
The band was playing swing
But Doctor Bop was rocking
With a boogie-woogie thing.

They told him play some dixie
They told him play some swing
But Doctor Bop just wouldn't stop
That boogie-woogie thing —

'Cause he had hot stuff, cool stuff
Good old break-the-rules stuff
Stuff with jelly, stuff with jam
Boogie-woogie stuff with a sis-boom-bam!

The Faithful Donut
(Slowly, with feeding)

FAR across the ocean,
    Far across the sea,
A faithful jelly donut
    Is waiting just for me.

Its sugar shines with longing,
    Its jelly glows with tears;
My donut has been waiting there
    For twenty-seven years.

O faithful jelly donut,
    I beg you, don't despair!
My teeth are in Toronto, but
    My heart is with you there.

And I will cross the ocean,
    And I will cross the sea,
And I will crush you to my lips,
    And make you one with me.

I wish I was a chocolate bar / A-sitting on a shelf / I'd stop and stare, with loving care, / And then I'd eat myself.

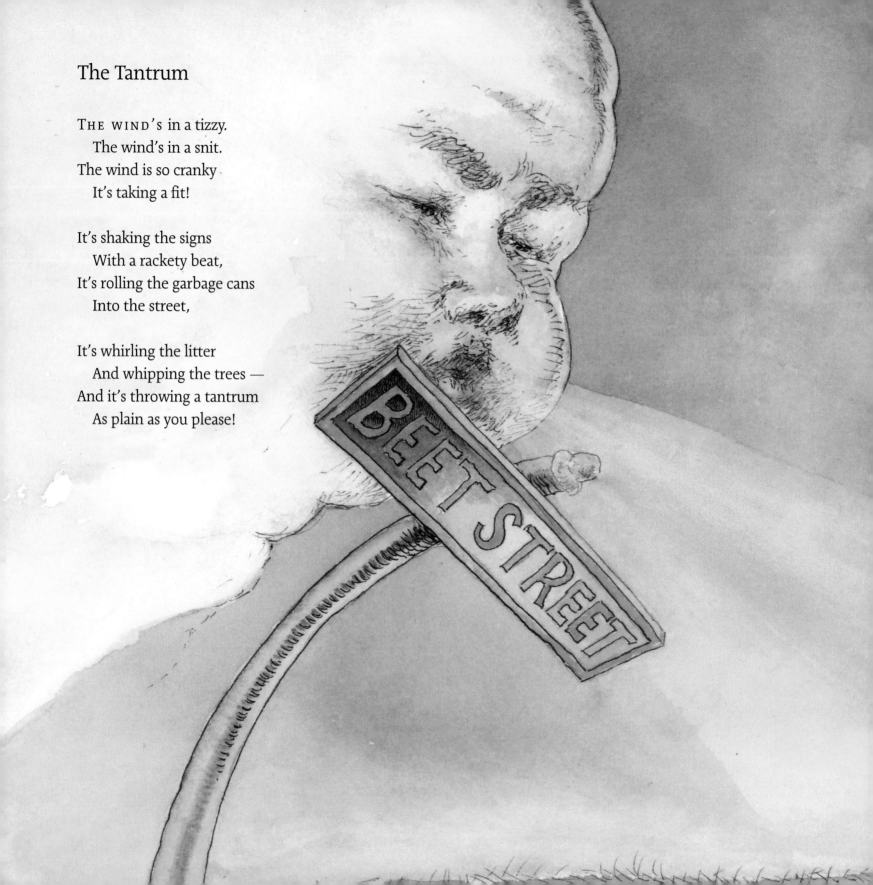

The Tantrum

THE WIND'S in a tizzy.
    The wind's in a snit.
The wind is so cranky
    It's taking a fit!

It's shaking the signs
    With a rackety beat,
It's rolling the garbage cans
    Into the street,

It's whirling the litter
    And whipping the trees —
And it's throwing a tantrum
    As plain as you please!

Bugs and beetles, don't be late,
Set your feelers nice and straight:
Puke the slimy crud you chewed,
And smear it through the humans' food.

Indigo Stallion

DEEPER than daylight,
    When evening has spread,
The indigo stallion
    Appears at your bed.

You're up, and you're off
    With the wind in your hair —
The indigo stallion
    Can fly through the air!

He carries you high
    And he carries you wide
On a supergalactical
    Indigo ride;

He carries you far
    To the land by the sea,
Then he brings you home safely
    To Mommy and me.

With a *bing* and a *bang* and a *boom*,
The witch is riding her broom.
The goblins are out, the ghosts are about,
With a *bing* and a *bang* and a *BOOM!*

Dead Men in Edmonton

DEAD men in Edmonton
Lie very still,
Dead men in Edmonton
Under the hill.

Some by a fever, and
Some by a chill —
Dead men in Edmonton
Lie very still.

(They know a secret, and
One day we will:
Dead men in Edmonton,
Under the hill.)

The Bully

He's a bully,
He's a bully,
'Cause his under-
Wear is woolly,

And his nose is
Like a pulley —
He's a bully-
Bully-o!

*Away down deep
In the belly of the beast,
A bully met a bully
At the bully-boy feast.*

*They bullied to the west.
They bullied to the east.
They bullied till the bully boys
Were both de-ceased!*

You bug me, slug, you bug me. / You bug me all day long. / So tug your coiff and bug right off, / Before I do you wrong.

He's a bully,
He's a bully,
And his under-
Wear is woolly —

See him push and
See him pully,
He's a bully-
Bully-o!

The New TV

I ORDERED a TV -vee-vee,
To see what I could see-see-see.
But the only thing that came-came-came
Was a big box with my name-name-name.

My friend said, "What a dit-dit-dit,
You have to open it-it-it!"
But the only thing I spied-spied-spied
Was another box inside-side-side.

My friend said, "You're so dim-dim-dim,
You have to plug it in-in-in!"
But all that could be seen-seen-seen
Was the big black empty screen-screen-screen.

My friend said, "What a jerk-jerk-jerk,
Press ON to make it work-work-work!"
But the only thing that showed-showed-showed
Was a coloured square that glowed-glowed-glowed.

My friend said, "It's too late-late-late,
Till morning you must wait-wait-wait."
So then we fell asleep-sleep-sleep
And lay in slumber deep-deep-deep.

But in the night a thief-thief-thief
To my dismay and grief-grief-grief
Made off with that TV -vee-vee,
So I never got to see-see-see...

Well now I sit alone-lone-lone
Inside my little home-home-home,
And in the evening glow-glow-glow
I watch the radio-o-o.

My brain is like the rain in Spain
That drains upon the waiting plain.
And every time it makes a stain,
I mop the darn thing up again.

I Remember, I Remember

I REMEMBER, I remember
How we used to play outside,
Running through the tall grass
Finding where to hide,

Chugging through the summertime
Like summer couldn't end:
That's the way we used to play,
Me and my old friend.

If Lonesome Was a Pot of Gold

IF LONESOME was a pot of gold,
    I'd be a millionaire.
If missing you was party time,
    I wouldn't have a care.

And if a flock of memories
    Could make a person sing,
I'd be an all-night radio
    And play like anything.

(It's not as though I dream about
    The things we used to do;
It's only morning, noon, and night
    I sit and think of you.)

Lavender and Bergamot

SWEET perfume in my garden grows:
Lavender and bergamot, jasmine, rose,

Sandalwood and juniper, ylang ylang —
Balm for the bee, and the heart's deep pang.

ROSE

BUG
SIGNS

MY FATHER WAS A KILLER BEE,
MY MOTHER WAS A BAT,
MY UNCLE WAS A WARTY TOAD,
AND THAT'S WHY I'M A BRAT.

Blue Balloon

NOBODY noticed,
    And nobody knew,
How lonely my heart
    In its little house grew,

When my friend went away,
    Yes, my friend went away —
My very best friend
    Went away to stay.

With a hullabaloo in a blue balloon:
Sing hey for my very best friend.

Now no one has noticed,
    And nobody knows,
How giddy my heart
    In its little house grows,

For it happened today,
    Yes, it happened today —
My very best friend
    Came home to stay!

With a hullabaloo in a blue balloon:
Sing hey for my very best friend!

Cuddle a bug in a towel,
Cuddle a bug in a rug.
Cuddle a bug in her own little bed,
Till she's snug in a big bug-hug.

You Too Lie Down

OVER every elm, the
      half-light hovers.
Down, you lie down too.
Through every shade of dusk, a hush
      impinges. Robins
settle to the nest; beneath, the deep earth
breathes, it
         breathes. You too lie
down, the drowsy room is
close and come to darkness.
            Hush, you
too can sleep at last. You
        too lie down.